The Andromedans

& Other Parables of Science and Faith

Denis Osborne

InterVarsity Press
Downers Grove
Illinois 60515

InterVarsity Press is the book-publishing division
of Inter-Varsity Christian Fellowship, a
student movement active on campus at hundreds
of universities, colleges and schools of
nursing. For information about local and regional
activities, write IVCF, 233 Langdon St.,
Madison, WI 53703.

Distributed in Canada through InterVarsity Press,
1875 Leslie St., Unit 10, Don Mills, Ontario
M3B 2M5, Canada.

Biblical quotations are from the Revised
Standard Version of the Bible, copyrighted 1946
and 1952. The extracts in chapter 18 are the
author's paraphrase.

ISBN 0-87784-600-6
Library of Congress Catalog
Card Number: 78-18550

Printed in the United States of America

This way and that way

Do you ever wonder what life is all about? Has science the answer? Or religion? Is there a God? Is there anything after death? Did Jesus rise from the dead and could those unlikely-seeming miracles ever have happened?

Perhaps you're more cynical. Some say that questions like these are irrelevant, meaningless and uninteresting for 'modern' men and women.

If you ask questions about life this short book is for you. If you've given up asking, it's still for you, for it may show that there are questions that we need to ask. The questioning cannot be repressed for ever. This is not a book of answers, though it is written with the conviction that questions should be asked and that some answers can be found.

There are times when life is like a maze. We rush this way and that way in our intellectual pursuits and in the busy-ness of living.
  Why are we here?
  Is there a way out?

The silence of science

Nebula in the constellation of Andromeda (Hale Observatories, Pasadena)

1. The Andromedans

The Andromedan spacemen had returned home after a long and arduous mission to planet Earth. When the mission leader was interviewed for Television Andromedia he claimed that his crew's ability to make themselves invisible had made it easy to study the planet without interference. He doubted whether Earthlings even knew of their visit.

While he spoke the TV cameras panned across a large and varied collection of trophies brought back from Earth: rocks and plants, dead animals, clothes, household goods and even a small car. The Andromedans were specially interested in the things made and used by the dominant species of Earthlings. 'Surely these Earthmen would have guessed that they had visitors from space when their possessions disappeared,' said one of the reporters questioning the Andromedan spaceman. In reply he said that he thought even the most intelligent species found on Earth both ignorant and untrustworthy. They would attribute such losses to natural causes or to the perversity of their fellows.

After his broadcast all the samples were rushed to Andromedan laboratories for careful and prolonged tests. One subject studied in detail was a newspaper. The chemists reported its composition, using Andromedan names for paper and ink.

'Is that all?' asked the leader of the space mission.

'Yes.'

'But they gave them to each other and said they were "The News".'

The chemists went back to their laboratories to carry out a further analysis and reported back to the mission leader.

'Nonsense. We don't know what Earthmen mean by news, nor do we know its chemical formula. But we are sure that there isn't any of this news stuff here. We have used our most accurate techniques and we have found that the mass of the ink plus the mass of the paper adds up to the total mass of the page. There is paper and ink; nothing more.'

So the news never reached Andromeda.

2 Why parables?

How do physicists explain the behaviour of gases? By a kinetic theory which, in its simplest form, likens the molecules of gas to perfectly elastic balls. One modification of the theory, for diatomic gases, pictures pairs of molecules taking a share of the total energy for their rotation and vibration. Descriptions and explanations in science make use of similarities and analogies in ways like these. Even if the treatment is mathematical the same type of thinking by analogy lies behind it. We construct a model in our imagination and change it until it would behave in the same way as the system that we are studying. It is important that the predictions based on the model should agree, in every way that can be tested, with observation and experiment in the real world. Indeed, if the theory makes one false prediction it must be rejected or modified. Outside science there is a long tradition of conveying ideas by analogy and also by allegory, stories in which each detail has some hidden meaning.

A parable usually differs from an analogy, and from an allegory, by having only one point of contact between a story told in familiar terms and the ideas which are its real concern. A parable is not like a scientific model in which there are parallels for every detail. A parable need not be a whole story: it may be just a simple metaphor or simile. Parables are helpful when we talk of things which are on the borders of our present experience. They are carriers for new ideas.

Some may argue that this seems an indirect approach. Why not speak clearly and directly rather than in parables? Partly because people may not listen: detailed arguments have little appeal until interest has been aroused and parables may suggest things that are worthy of careful study later on. But really we can't help using parables however hard we try. If we are to describe something that is new to people, outside their present experience, we have to compare and contrast it with the things they know. Our description will take familiar words and use them in a new way. The language of science gives many examples of everyday words that have acquired a new meaning, words such as force, work, wave and information.

Others may argue against the deliberate use of parables, that this is cheating if it makes complicated things appear simpler than they are. There is some force in this objection, especially if a parable is confused with an argument from analogy, where it is supposed that because things have some similar attributes we may expect their other features to be similar. It is not the function of a parable to serve instead of detailed and thorough study. Parables should suggest new approaches to old problems, and sometimes new problems to be faced.

We shall use parables in this book, not only story-parables but also short similes and diagrams. The aim is to sow the seeds of new ideas rather than to explore subjects in detail. Some parables are explained; some are better left unexplained so that we 'see the truth' for ourselves. A good parable should be worth reading, or telling, more than once.

On some subjects there is good precedent for speaking in parables!

∃ The three brothers

'Why do the hands of my watch go round?' Bob asked. His elder brother, a technician, opened the watch and explained the functions of the different parts that they could see. Bob had studied physics and thought he understood his brother's explanation with its references to resonance in a quartz crystal and electronic circuitry. Bob now knew all he wanted to know about his watch.

Bob wanted to boast about his new-found knowledge and asked his younger brother the same question, 'Why do the hands of my watch go round?'

The answer came more quickly than he expected. 'To tell you the time, stupid.'

Bob was not so much stupid as confused, for he had used the word 'Why?' when he meant to ask 'How?' But he got the answer he expected when told about the mechanism of the watch rather than its purpose. Bob was not alone in confusing questions about why things happen with questions about how they work.

4, *Complementarity*

Is light a wave or is light a particle? This question confronted physicists in the 1920s. Diffraction and interference effects, they thought, had proved it to be a wave, but studies on scattering showed that it was 'really' a stream of particles, like bullets from a machine-gun. It was then suggested that particles of matter might show the properties of waves and it was found experimentally that a stream of electrons, small particles of matter, could produce the diffraction patterns that were characteristic of wave motion. The analogies had broken down. Waves like those on the sea would not be scattered by obstacles in the way that light was scattered, nor could billiard balls be expected to show the wave properties that had been found with a stream of electrons.

The Danish physicist, Niels Bohr, accepted the apparent contradiction and used the word *complementarity* to describe the fact that light behaved in some interactions as a wave and in others as a particle. The difficulties experienced by physicists about the wave-particle duality of things are largely forgotten today. We recognize that waves and particles, and the mathematics associated with them, are only 'models'. We shouldn't say 'light is a wave' or 'light is a particle', but rather 'light behaves like a wave' or 'like a particle'. We have got used to the idea that the actual behaviour of light is inadequately described by either analogy on its own.

The concept of complementarity in physics interested philosophers and theologians, acting as a reminder that more than one type of study is necessary if we are to understand the whole. We can design experiments to study light as a form of wave motion, or as a stream of particles. We can make a chemical analysis of a printed page, or we can read its message. We can ask about the working of a watch, or about its purpose. When we have information of different types we may speak about *complementary* sets of facts. Facts of the same set, such as a more detailed chemical analysis of a system for which the chemistry was already partly known, would be *supplementary* facts, giving us more information of the same type.

Complementarity is a one-word parable, taking an idea from physics and using it in other contexts. Many people have suggested that there is a complementary relationship between religious faith and scientific knowledge. Perhaps they are right.

5 Compatibility

The information about a building provided by a plan and an elevation is complementary. We cannot deduce details about one from our knowledge of the other. Given the plan of a house we could never be sure what it looked like. Conversely, given a photograph we would remain in doubt about the floor plan and the number of rooms in the building.

But if we see the photograph of a modest suburban home we do not imagine that the plans will be those of a castle. The plan and the elevation must 'fit' if they are both truthful descriptions of the same building. More generally, complementary truths must be *compatible* with each other. A chemical analysis will not help us to discover the meaning of a printed page, but the chemical properties of the system determine whether or not it can act as a memory to store any information at all (for the printed page to serve its purpose the ink must be a different colour from the paper and must dry without getting smudged). It is foolish to confuse 'why?' questions and 'how?' questions about a watch or any other piece of machinery, but a competent engineer may be able to guess the purpose of a machine even if he has never seen anything like it before.

Given two sets of facts that are supposed to be complementary, we can subject them to the text of compatibility. The compatibility of two descriptions of the same system is no proof that either is true, but their incom-

A circle is the ground plan of some of these solids and not others. From a circular plan alone we cannot discover which solid is intended, but two of them can be eliminated at once as incompatible.

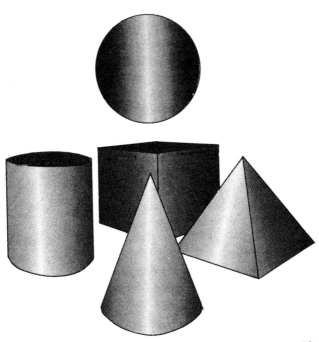

19

patibility would show that one of them, at least, must be rejected. This holds for the relationship between science and faith. The idea of complementarity does not remove science and religion into two unconnected realms. We are not free to believe what we choose in religion without reference to science, nor free to do what we will in science and its application without concern for the moral imperatives of religion. Our religious beliefs should be in harmony with our understanding of the natural world. The need for compatibility acts as a constraint and a guide.

Animism, the belief that different aspects of nature are controlled by independent deities who respond capriciously to men's requests and offerings, seems incompatible with the belief about the uniformity of nature that underlies scientific study. By the same test we may also cast doubt on many other religions. Of course we must approach this with some caution and humility: the wave and particle theories characteristic of light were thought at first to be contradictory.

6 Nothing-buttery

What is the next letter in the sequence,

A C F J ?

Easy. Taking the alphabet in sequence the gaps between the letters are one letter, two letters, three letters. The next letter in the sequence is **O**.

Try another. What is the next letter in this sequence,

B C D G J ?

If you have been brought up on mathematical series or sequences you may get it wrong, or you may get it right for the wrong reason. The letters in this sequence are those for which the shape of the capitals as printed includes a part that is curved! The next letter in the sequence is **O**, followed of course by **P, Q, R** and **S**.

There are blinkers on our thinking. We investigate one particular line while other possibilities are forgotten. Everything we learn raises new questions in our minds, but these questions are attempts to elicit further information of the type known already. We need to remember that studies of one type, however sophisticated, may not lead us to other aspects of a problem which are equally interesting and important. A study of chemistry may convince us that our bodies are 'nothing but' an ordering of different chemicals. True, but chemical systems may have a meaning and significance that the study of chemistry can never disclose. There is a deep misunderstanding behind the assertion that because the human body is only a chemical system it cannot have

. . . definite changes in his behaviour.

more significance than an amoeba or a piece of rock.

Suppose we are told that a man is 'in love'. Those who knew him before would observe definite changes in his behaviour, although they had never met the girl. Such changes could be studied carefully and made the subject of a detailed physiological and psychological report. If these studies were made without ever seeing the girl we might imagine that the biochemical changes observed were themselves an explanation for the man's emotions. Perhaps he is mentally sick, 'in love' with a female who does not exist. He needs this relationship; may not the need itself have led him to invent a woman in the recesses of his subconscious?

Another man claims to believe in God. Some of his friends, who knew him before his conversion, will testify to his change in life-style. But they wonder if his faith arises from a quest for a father-substitute or satisfies some other deep internal needs. His faith, they say, is nothing but an internal psychological state or nothing but a response to his social environment.

Of course they could be right. One man may have delusions about God just as another may be 'in love' with a girl who exists only in his dreams. But their suspicions may be unfounded. They may be guilty of 'nothing-buttery'. They could meet the girl, if they knew where to find her. Could they also meet God?

7 Gaps

There are a number of traditional arguments for belief in a God. I do not find any of them wholly convincing. Oh yes, I *do* believe in God (I'm sure you had guessed that already), but any arguments that claim to present God to us as the conclusion to some chain of reasoning hardly seem to do him justice. Some of the arguments raised in his defence are clearly false. False arguments do not necessarily lead to false conclusions, but they could be so disheartening to those 'feeling after God' that they deserve a little thought.

One family of false arguments is of the type, 'because we cannot understand this, God must have done it'. Anything from the colouring of a butterfly to the complexity of the human eye, or from the coincidences of history to the complex pattern of stellar evolution has been quoted as a reason why men ought to believe in God. These are nonsense arguments. They are unscientific: the limitations in our present knowledge are no reason why we should use 'God' as an explanation. They are illogical: why should we think that God is somehow more active in matters of which we are ignorant than in those which we understand? They are unchristian: a god who has been invented to hide our ignorance is not a real God at all but a construction of the human mind, a mental equivalent to those idols of former generations made in wood and stone. Such attempts to fit God into the gaps in our knowledge are also most unfortunate, for, as science grows, the gaps get smaller and the god that fills them must get smaller too.

Attempts to defend the Christian faith by arguing for a 'God in the gaps' of our knowledge did justice to neither faith nor science but produced attitudes that have conditioned the thinking of our age. Perhaps this is why some people fear that a discussion of evolution is somehow dangerous for the Christian and why the discovery of 'missing links' between animals and men are hailed as victories against religious belief. Perhaps this is why some people think that if life were created in a test-tube it would somehow discredit faith in God or why they expect the discovery of intelligent beings elsewhere in the universe to be an embarrassment to the Christian believer.

Behind these false arguments, and the folly of the 'God in the gaps' defence of religious belief, there lies the error of nothing-buttery. Against this we must assert that to explain something does not mean to explain it away. Explanation at one level does not rule out the possibility of a different and equally valid explanation at another level. We need to assert the existence of complementary truths, remembering that a chemical analysis will not tell us the message on a page of print or the significance of a human relationship.

Between science and faith we may rightly ask that the interpretation of experience given by science and the interpretation given by religion should be compatible. But we would not expect to deduce our scientific knowledge of the natural world from our religious beliefs and we would be equally foolish if we expected to acquire a faith in God through our scientific activity.

II

Doubting the impossible

*In PART I we have seen that many things are **possible**, although they might be **invisible** from a viewpoint within the traditions of modern science because our total knowledge may have many complementary parts. That does not leave us free to believe anything we choose: some things are incompatible and ought not to be believed.*

In PART II we ask what we can believe. Can we accept the miraculous? Could there be life after death? Is there any evidence that will convince us, one way or the other, on questions such as these? The answers to these questions are fundamental to our understanding of nature, to all the decisions we must make and to all our relationships.

8 *Flatland*

Flatland is a world of two dimensions. People in Flatland move around and see things only on the surface of their two-dimensional space. They have knowledge of north and south, and of east and west, but not of up and down. The story of Flatland was written by Edwin Abbott and first published in 1884.

Abbott was a mathematician and he used the symbolism of geometry to ridicule the class structure of human society. Flatland people are class-ified by shape. The aristocrats are circles, the working classes triangles and the soldiers irregular triangles with acutely angled vertices that can inflict great damage in battle. (The author claimed for himself the middle-class status of a 'square' long before the name had its present significance.) In Flatland a woman is a straight line: the front end contains the eye and is luminous but the rear is both dark and sharp, a dagger-like hazard by which she can stab to death any man who inadvertently stumbles into her! Abbott pursued this satire on sexual prejudice. It is because of the danger that women present to men that by law in Flatland members of the 'thinner sex' have been made to develop a rhythmical and well-modulated undulation of the back when in company so that they can be seen more readily.

Flatland houses are pentagonal. Their walls are lines but the inhabitants of Flatland cannot stand outside or see things beyond their two-dimensional space and they can no more see through a line than we can see through a solid wall.

One day a sphere came near to Flatland. First, he spoke to people from above. But they didn't know there was such a thing as an 'above' that was different from north and were bothered because they could not see anyone although they heard a voice. The unseen visitor claimed that he could see them and look right into their houses even when the doors and windows were closed. 'To me your inside is the same as your outside.' Then he moved into Flatland itself. Of course the Flatlanders saw only a circle that grew steadily bigger and bigger as

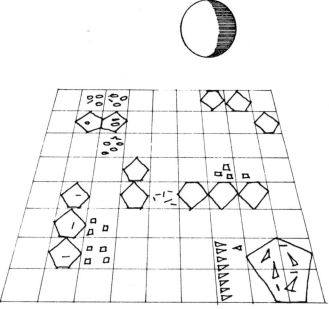

the sphere descended, reaching its maximum size when he was half-way through the Flatland plane. He made several visits, appearing sometimes inside a locked and shuttered room before vanishing again into nothing.

The author claims that, as a square in Flatland, he heard and saw the sphere and was transported temporarily into a three-dimensional world. He told his friends about his discovery and tried to preach to them a gospel of three dimensions, a gospel that made it possible for mere squares to understand much that was previously inexplicable and that offered an experience of life that was exciting and full because it was free from the constraints of Flatland. But he met with ridicule and was imprisoned for his dangerous teaching. The Flatlanders were sure that something inconceivable, in their limited two-dimensional frame, was also impossible.

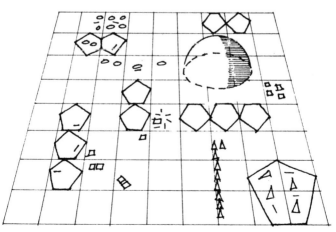

Telepathy:
The physicist's problem

The evidence given in support of telepathy suggests a method of communication between persons that can:

(*1*) *carry detailed information;*
(*2*) *be subject to error or disturbance;*
(*3*) *span distances up to thousands of kilometers;*
(*4*) *occur instantaneously (travelling with the velocity of light would do!);*
(*5*) *occur independently of any of the traditionally recognized human senses.*

The energy used by the brain is not large and it follows that the energy available for telepathic communication must be very much less than the energies normally used in radio communication. The intensity of any signal decreases with distance, an inverse square law, and the signal is lost when its intensity is at about the same level as the background noise.

The background noise cannot be avoided. It is less at low temperatures but the temperature of a human receiver is not low. It is less at low frequencies and if a low-energy signal is to be detected at great distances it must be of very low frequency. But for such signals the rate at which information can be carried is small, not enough to give the detail claimed for telepathy. At low frequencies the number of channels available is small and if there were many transmitters it would be impossible to distinguish one transmission from another. The problem is analogous to that of tuning a radio receiver when two or more stations are transmitting on nearly the same frequency. With some four thousand million humans their telepathic signals, if any, would get hopelessly jammed.

The physical principles behind these arguments are those such as the inverse square law and the equipartition of energy. They determine the relationship between noise level and frequency, the rate at which information can be carried by a channel and the band width of that channel. They are general principles. Even if there is some means of communication unknown to us at present, just as electromagnetic waves were unknown until near the end of the nineteenth century, physicists would expect the same principles to apply.

It certainly looks as though telepathy is impossible!

⁊ An open mind

Having an open mind is considered praiseworthy, but there is much confusion about what this means.

Take an example: does telepathy really happen? Some say it *cannot*; others say it *does*. What is the evidence? There are reports of many experiments, with card sequences for example, that provide a statistical basis for thinking that there is some means of communication between minds independent of the recognized channels of sense. But there are also objections to the idea: it not only goes beyond what is known already but seems to contradict present knowledge (see the separate note on telepathy and physics). At the time of writing the evidence for telepathy is inconclusive and the objections to the idea are such that we ought to examine any fresh evidence very carefully before accepting it.

We may think that there is evidence in our own individual experience. Don't other people sometimes say just what *you* have been thinking? But are we sure that these coincidences are more than random? Even if we can guess the thoughts of our friends fairly often we may wonder if there is some explanation for this, other than telepathy. It may be a simple one: John always wriggles his ears when thinking of Mary, so that when we see John's ears wriggling we associate this with Mary without consciously identifying the signal.

It would be unscientific and unconvincing if we made extravagant claims based on the interpretation of our individual experience. But it would be equally unscientific to assert that telepathy is impossible just because we cannot conceive any mechanism to explain it. That would be Flatlander thinking. Some of the alleged proofs and demonstrations of telepathy have been fakes but that does not disprove the possibility of the 'real thing'. The right attitude is, surely, one of enquiry. We should have an open mind on the question.

Many people would profess to have an open mind on the occurrence of telepathy. If they were later convinced by further evidence would their minds be less open than before and would their attitude then be less creditable? If so, it would make a virtue of ignorance and indecision. One can imagine, for example, experimental results providing firm evidence for telepathy. If our minds were really open to such evidence we would be convinced, for the open mind will not necessarily remain an empty mind.

There are people who claim that they 'keep an open mind' on other questions but who are not really open to conviction. They are keeping empty minds, minds that are open at both ends so that any truth is lost as fast as it is found. Their claim to keep an open mind is an excuse for indecision. By contrast, the man with a truly open mind is ready to accept new evidence supporting revolutionary ideas even when these seem to contradict present knowledge. He is open to conviction. Perhaps describing a mind as 'open' fosters misunderstanding. The concept of an open mind is static, of something waiting to be filled. Mental activity is better described in more dynamic terms: we enquire, search, test and explore. It is the virtues of an enquiring mind that we should prize, not just an open mind and passive receptivity. It was the enquiring minds of Einstein and Planck and others that introduced a new era in physics and brought the recognition that the physical world is a place much more exciting, and much less 'solid', than any nineteenth-century physicist had dreamed of.

10 *The book and the body*

A man is like a book.

A book is 'nothing but' paper and ink and yet it carries information. The information can be lost if the pages are torn or cut or if paint is spilt on them. The physical structure should not be confused with the information it carries, but the two are very closely related. A physical change can change the information contained on a page: you could alter the meaning of the last sentence if you cut out the word 'not' with a pair of scissors.

It is much the same with man. The effects of brain surgery, of electric-shock treatment and of drugs show a direct connection between a man's body and his personality. But it is not sufficient to describe a man only in the language of physics and chemistry even though we may change a man's character by an operation or modify his behaviour with drugs. Complex systems usually have an order, an information content, that makes it impossible for them to be described fully in terms of the basic sciences. We should expect that a system with the complexity of a human body will have some qualities different from those studied in physics or physiology, or even psychology or sociology, just as a book carries information that can never be discovered by chemistry. When we consider the relationship between two human beings we have a situation in which the complexity is 'squared' and we should not be surprised to find that the result is very complicated indeed. Our attempts to understand such relationships need not be unscientific but we should not expect to express the results adequately in the language of any of the sciences. That would be similar to the expectation that a chemical analysis could reveal the meaning of a printed page.

We live in an age that mixes its scepticism with credulity. Some people even believe the adverts on TV! Others show an amazing credulity in the pursuit of science, accepting claims about research results without questioning the motives of the research worker, or trusting the reports of statistical surveys without asking what they might mean. It is small wonder that some people seem willing to believe anything. There are those who rejoice in irrationality and no creed is too bizarre to win some adherents. But to hold mutually incompatible beliefs is another way of believing nothing.

Perhaps we can see much that is good in the revolt against 'science'. We do well to recognize the limits to our reasoning skills. It is good that many people are disenchanted with a mechanistic view of human life. It is good if the experience of personal relationships makes it impossible for us to treat other people as though they were 'ordinary' things. It is good if we have struggled enough in reaching decisions to find it difficult to accept a determinist view of human behaviour. But it is not good to abandon reason and rejoice in contradiction and absurdity. To deny the validity of reason is as inhuman as to exalt it at the expense of other factors that contribute to the richness and variety of life. The processes of reasoning are just as much a *part* of our experience as the feelings aroused by personal relationships and the need to take decisions.

Our interpretation of the different parts of experience requires a complementarity. We should not expect *deductive* links between the different aspects of knowledge and experience but our different beliefs should be compatible. Are the claims that are made about human freedom and responsibility, and the claims about the persistence of human consciousness beyond physical death, compatible with what we know about ourselves from other sources?

11. *Dead and buried*

Is death the end? It's hard to imagine what form life after death could take. A man's body dies. It decomposes and the whole system that sustained the thought processes and consciousness of the man is completely destroyed. Particular memories were associated, in life, with brain patterns and signals that exist no more. Can there be any meaningful continuity of existence without the memory store that gives personal identity? John Brown's body lies a-mouldering in the grave. What can it mean to claim that his soul is marching on?

Of course it is part of the Christian tradition to believe in a life after death and many people claim to hold such beliefs. Could it be wishful thinking, a projection of their unfulfilled ambitions into an imagined future? Could it be a form of escapism, of 'pie in the sky when we die', which enables men to avoid responsibility for social reforms which ought to be their present concern? Could it be an attempt to ensure conformity to certain moral attitudes with the threat that we shall be called to account for our present actions?

Despite the fashion for the occult most of our contemporaries think rather little about life after death and regard it as a fairy tale that is not to be believed by men who have come of age. Others may be less confident in their rejection of the idea but adopt a practical agnosticism: 'the troubles of this life are enough for me'.

There was a special book, a manuscript. Alas it was

thrown on a fire and burnt. The book and its message were destroyed. Was that the end of it?

It would have been, but knowing that there were vagabonds around who would try to burn the book I had read it aloud into a microphone and stored its message in a tape-recorder. The book was destroyed but not its message. Information that had been given in a pattern of ink on paper and communicated to me by light waves had been changed into a sequence of magnetic signals on tape ready for further conversion into electrical signals and sound waves. The same piece of information can take many different forms.

A man is like a book.

Of course there is also a great difference between men and books. The message of a book does not change with time; it is static. A man is dynamic, entering into relationships with other men and with his surroundings, changing them and being changed by them. However, if the message of a book could be recorded on tape, why should we think it impossible for the complex dynamic message, the significance or personality of a man to be given another form which could exist independently of his present body? We should be wrong to think, because of the close relationship between a man's body and personality, that life after death is impossible.

Perhaps we can take the comparison further. In order to make the message of the book available in another form it was necessary that someone should read it. The survival of the message depended on the reader. Jesus claimed that men could have eternal life because of their relationship to the eternal God. We should be foolish to imagine that *all* the old-fashioned talk about our souls should be regarded as nonsense. We do not need to think of the soul as something added to our bodies, like a bag of gas somehow trapped inside them, but it could describe us in our relationship with God. He knows us better than we know ourselves.

12 Goal!

There was tension in the crowd as they watched the soccer match. Some were keen fans of the game and understood what was going on. Even those who had never played in their lives had worked out something of the rules simply by watching it before. They had seen a superb drive, the ball was in the air and the goalkeeper in quite the wrong position. Those familiar with the game knew that this time it must certainly be a goal.

A bang, a flash, and sudden darkness.

The projector had fused and with that the ball, the goal and the players alike had vanished into nothingness. The path of the ball, which subconscious calculations based on past experience had shown must surely end in the goal, was no longer part of the scene, for the crowd had been watching a film and the real source of the whole sequence of events lay in the projector behind them.

Of course you could argue that the real source was the original soccer match from which the film had been made. There had been a real ball and in the real match a goal had been scored. But films can be made by means of cartoon drawings and the point of the story remains valid: the cause of each event watched by that crowd lay in something other than the events that went before.

The world could be like that, not necessarily just a 'projection' but a real world in which there are fundamental causes different from those that we see. We observe the world and in our sciences learn the rules of the game but there could be deeper rules that we do not know. The future is not necessarily determined by past events and we are naïve if we confuse the unexpected with the impossible. If we mean by miracle something inexplicable in ordinary terms we have no warrant from science to reject all accounts of the·miraculous without further enquiry. However we should not go to the other extreme and accept uncritically every fanciful story that we hear. If we read or hear about a miracle we should ask what happened, and why. Christians believe that there have been real miracles and that they are signs from God, intended to make us think.

Christians should not fear attempts to explain the miraculous, for the unusual can be an effective sign of God's working whether we understand the mechanism or not. One possible mechanism that could account for many miracles arises from the indeterminate character of individual events as understood in physics. These indeterminate events are all of a very small scale. For example, we have no way of finding out in which direction an individual photon of light energy will be emitted from an atom. We cannot predict when an individual radioactive nucleus will disintegrate. Because we deal normally with systems in which millions of these events occur we are not bothered by the impossibility of predicting each one, we are content with averages. But the statistically unusual would not involve any breaking of the 'rules'. Perhaps God has chosen to work miracles not as special interventions contrary to the natural order of things but as special manifestations of his normal control of the world. Such ideas must be treated with some caution lest we try to install God in the gaps of an ignorance due to 'indeterminacy'. However, it seems right to ask ourselves how we think God is related to his world and to give answers in terms of the accepted world-view of our age, though it does not follow that this will give us an argument with which to convince others that they ought to believe in God.

But how is God normally active in his world? The Bible describes him as upholding the universe by his word of power. Those who believe in God can regard every quantum jump as an act of God and recognize in the statistical regularity of the physical world a witness to God's integrity (which is part of his holiness) on which all scientific knowledge depends.

A God who sustains the universe? A God who can work miracles? These are tremendous claims and perhaps you are asking whether there *is* a God and how we can know this. It is to these questions that we turn next.

III.

Seeing and believing

13 *Nowhere?*

A nineteenth-century atheist was determined that his daughter should not acquire any mistaken religious ideas as she grew up. He knew that when she went into the homes of some of her school friends she would see Bible texts hanging on the walls, for such was the fashion of the age. To counter this he hung in their living room, while the girl was still very young and not yet able to read, an anti-text that read simply:

GOD IS
NOWHERE

Some months later the little girl surprised her father by telling him that she could read 'the writing on the wall'. Proudly, slowly and syllable-by-syllable as a young child might, she said, 'God is now here.'

But the story has a double edge. It is possible to realize that God is 'now here' only if it is also true that he is 'no where'. If God were limited to one place at one time he would not be in every place at every time.

Do you ever wonder about God? Because God is no 'where' the task of looking for him differs from any other search that we might make. When Paul the Apostle spoke to the philosophers in Athens he told them about men feeling after God and finding him and went on to say, 'Yet he is not far from each one of us,' and to quote from a Greek writer:

'In him we live and move and have our being.'

1L The dreamer

Can we be sure about anything?

Three months ago you were riding in a car. Suddenly there was a crash which you cannot remember. You were rushed to hospital unconscious and have not yet regained consciousness. Everything that you think has happened in the past three months has been a dream.

Now *prove* me wrong! I don't think you can.

Have you not felt at times, 'This can't be happening, I must be dreaming'? Perhaps you have even wondered if the whole of life is a dream that you enjoy, or suffer, in splendid isolation. It could be argued that if the whole of life was a dream we would not be able to distinguish, as we do, between dreaming and waking; but that argument cannot kill the idea that our sensations might be only a dream-like experience of things that do not have any independent existence of their own. Some drugs blur the boundary between reality and the inner world of dreams and some forms of mysticism value experiences that are divorced from the physical environment. So what is real? Normally we take it for granted that we live within a real environment and that we can change that environment by our actions. But once we question this it becomes very hard to get any answer to our question, for the question itself casts doubt on a presupposition on which all reasoning and argument is based.

Some men have been troubled by this inability to prove, in the way that they would wish, that things exist

'Perhaps I'm really a man who thinks he is a caterpillar, who thinks he is a . . .?'

independently and externally to themselves. I won't debate what is meant by the existence of a chair or the existence of an electron but I want to suggest that we all make a presupposition about other people: that they exist and that they have thoughts and feelings somewhat like our own. We grow up to accept this as a basis for thought and action, of course, and only a specious reasoning would question its validity.

Surely:

> We believe in other people,
> our brothers and sisters in the human race,
> our equals,
> with whom we share the custody of planet Earth.
> We may not trust them,
> we may not like them,
> but we believe that they are real.

We can't prove their existence in the way that we prove things in mathematics. They could be just phantoms in our dreams or products of our fevered brains, invented by us and made in our image. But despite that logical possibility we do believe. The belief is not simply rational, for it serves as a basis for reasoning and cannot be justified by the process of deduction. But unbelief would be unreasonable! The whole of our experience counts as evidence for the validity of this faith. This is something we are sure about (unless we are sick in mind or under the influence of drugs). We take the reality of other people as proven even though there is no deductive argument to show that this is so.

What do people want when they ask for some proof of the existence of God? Usually they seek some proof of the deductive type used in mathematics, that A implies B implies C. They want something like Pythagoras' theorem but ending with 'therefore God exists'. They might think the Christian evasive when he says that you can't prove God's existence that way, but if one limits the idea of proof to deductive arguments alone then proofs of existence don't exist. It is equally impossible to prove the existence of a friend.

There is evidence about God that convinces many thinking men and women. I believe that God exists as firmly as I believe that my wife exists. If you demand some deductive argument in support of this I cannot give it to you; I cannot prove to you the reality of either of them in a way that will compel you to believe. Even if you met my wife you might think it was just a dream. I did when I first fell in love with her.

15 *People and things*

There is a difference between knowing things and knowing people. We find out about things by *our* observations; but we find out about people by *their* words and actions. Of course most of our knowledge about anything and everybody is second hand, by report from others, but I am concerned here with knowledge that we get directly for ourselves.

Suppose I want to describe a car to you. I can tell you about its make and model, its colour, its top speed and its acceleration under different conditions. I can give you the measurements for its length and its weight and give a rather more subjective description of its handling characteristics. All of this information could be gained by the measurements and the road tests that I made myself.

But now suppose I want to tell you about its owner. I might measure his height and weight, take a photograph and study his behaviour. But in this way I would not find out very much about him as a man. If I limited my report to the results of these observations my description of him would be sadly lacking in the more important aspects of his humanity. In order to know about his hopes and fears, the things he thinks about and what he is really like as a man, I would need to hear him speak. If he did not speak to me himself I might learn something about him from others, but that would depend on his having spoken to them.

Our knowledge of people depends on what they do (by communicating with us or with others), while our knowledge of things depends on what we do. In practice there may be much in common between the study of things and of people; the psychiatrist knows how to elicit a response from his patient and the good teacher can provoke his students. The difference between observation and self-disclosure need not be pressed to extremes for the distinction to be valid. There are some facts about other people that we can know by observation, whether they like it or not, but in general the more our knowledge depends on *our* investigations alone the more closely it corresponds to knowing somebody as a thing.

There's another distinctive feature about knowing a person. It's a two-way business: I know him and he knows me. A personal relationship is something very different from our knowledge of a car. The distinction is more obvious in French than in English with *connaître* and *savoir* indicating different types of knowledge.

And God? Christians claim that God is personal. It is consistent with this to claim that God will be known through his self disclosure in a way that a person is known, and that God knows us. We should not be surprised to find that natural science has little help to give when we ask questions about God and his purposes.

16 *Personality plus*

We say that a snail is alive and that a man is alive without implying that men are no more lively than snails. In the same way the description of God as a personal being would not limit him to personality in our own likeness. What do we mean by God? Certainly not something less than ourselves. We are not free to invent any God that we choose, for such a God would be no God at all. We are asking if there is a real God, a being 'behind' the universe and yet a God who is now here. The degree of organization and complexity in a God responsible for the universe must be much greater than the complexity of a human body. We would expect this God to be more than personal, not impersonal. The knowledge of this God would depend on his self-disclosure rather than on our enquiries alone.

Christians claim that God had a purpose in creation and that his concern for men is that we should enter into a new relationship with him and with each other. Anyone who admits that this *might* be true must surely recognize that it is supremely important to become sure whether it is true or not. Otherwise one could miss the very point of living, and stumble purposelessly to the grave alienated from God, from human society as it is meant to be and from the whole of creation.

The search for God might well start, for a man of any culture, from the study of those religions which claim to bring a revelation from a personal God to men. Three of the world's major religions make this claim. They are all in the same 'family', Judaism, Christianity and Islam. There is not time here to examine their distinctive claims in detail but the reader who is interested may like to read *The world's religions* edited by Sir Norman Anderson (IVP).

17 *The picture in the snow*

Some children's books have puzzle pictures in which animals or faces are hidden in the drawing. If one turns the book round and keeps searching the picture for a time, one would see several rabbits in the trees or in the tangled weeds below. Once one has 'seen' the hidden objects they are nearly always immediately apparent when looking at the picture again even after an interval of several weeks.

There is a face in the pattern on page 55. It may take you some time to find it but once you have 'seen' it you will probably find that the face is there every time you look at the picture. If you can't find the face show it to someone else. Someone who has seen it can help you to find it too. The earliest report I can find about this pattern with the face was given by P. B. Porter in the *American Journal of Psychology* in 1954. It has caught the imagination of different people: being used by one to illustrate the principles of pattern recognition in a course on computing, and distributed by another in churches in the United States with a note explaining its religious significance. The religious story told about the picture is of a Chinese photographer, feeling very troubled, who took a photo of the melting snow with black earth showing through. As the print developed he was amazed to see the face of Christ, full of tenderness and love, and he became a Christian. I am not sure whether this story is a pious

invention or whether it was thought necessary to suppress any mention of such a suspect origin before publication in a scientific journal!

Whatever the truth about the picture, it illustrates the point: faith may be likened to recognition. The Christian believer looks at the same world and reads the same Bible as the man who rejects the Christian faith. But the Christian has recognized something special, something unique in Jesus Christ that makes him acknowledge Jesus Christ as Lord. In likening faith to recognition I am not trying to suggest how faith differs from other forms of 'knowing' but how it is that different people, looking at the same things, can interpret them in totally different ways. It is possible for someone who sees things in one way to undergo a change of mind and come to a completely different understanding about them. This happens when the puzzle picture is recognized as a face. I have found something similar happening when solving problems in mathematics. I might discover the right approach after many hours of struggling and uncertainty. I would need to work hard, still, to obtain the full solution but while wrestling with the problem I had come to a moment when I knew 'this is the way'.

In mathematics, as in our ideas about religion, it is possible to be mistaken and important that we allow others to correct us. Friends can help us find the right approach to a mathematical problem, or the pattern in a puzzle picture, and friends can help us to 'see' Christ.

When we recognize the special truth that there is in Jesus Christ we shall find that he awakens in us a response of trust and obedience. This is something more fundamental than the recognition of a pattern in a picture, or the discovery of the way to solve a mathematical problem, for it is something in which we are involved personally and completely. Christian faith differs from other types of knowledge because of the *content* of what is known. Knowing that God is now here and knowing something about this almighty God requires a greater level of commitment from us than anything else we can know. Once a man has recognized Jesus Christ as Lord he finds Christ everywhere in the pattern of life.

1❽ *Faith and recognition*

What is faith? Is it believing something without any justification? Is it an act of defiance and protest against a world where even our thoughts have to conform? Is it like an escape to the world of Hobbits or taking refuge on Watership Down? No. Christian faith is confidence in the God who has acted in history.

The New Testament writers understood faith as trust in Jesus Christ. What they said and wrote was intended as evidence that could lead men to trust him: but it could equally be explained away by those who were not willing to believe. If only men would think about it everything would fit together and they would recognize that Jesus Christ is Lord. It was just the same for those who met Jesus face-to-face as for those who heard of him in later years: faith was recognition.

*

'What do men say about me?'

'Oh, they say you're great. Like one of the old prophets with us again. Some even say you're really Elijah, or John the Baptizer.'

'What do you think?'

'You are the Christ,' said Peter, meaning the long expected deliverer and leader whom the Jews had expected God to send them.

*

Two men walked out of the city. Their leader had been executed; their colleagues had gone to ground. A stranger joined them and as they walked they told him what had happened to Jesus.

The stranger explained how the holy writings had predicted these things. People had rejected the prophets; of course they would reject the greatest prophet of all, the Christ.

'Stay with us,' they said, at journey's end, and he did. They sat down to supper. The stranger took some bread and said a prayer as he broke it; and they remembered. As they recognized him he vanished from their sight.

When they returned to Jerusalem they found their former colleagues together again, buzzing with excitement because they had been told already that Jesus was alive.

*

'Woman, why are you weeping? Who are you looking for?'

She thought he was the gardener who looked after the cemetery and said, 'If you've moved his body tell me where it is and I will take him away.'

'Mary.'

As soon as he spoke her name like that she knew him.

'Teacher,' she whispered in amazement, giving him his title.

He told her to tell the others and she ran, bursting with the news that Jesus had risen. 'I have seen him,' she said, 'I have seen the Lord.'

*

'You say you've seen the Lord? I'll not believe unless I can feel where the nails went when they killed him, and put my hand where they pierced his side with a sword,' said doubting Thomas.

'Reach your finger here, see my hands, put your hand in my wounds. Doubt no longer, but believe,' said Jesus to Thomas a week later.

So what did Thomas think? Did he say he was glad to find Jesus alive after all? He said much more than that, for he knew now what it meant. Thomas replied to Jesus, 'My Lord and my God!'

19 Two attitudes

Two students went to their laboratories. One was a brilliant young research fellow and the other a struggling first-year student. It was their habit while waiting for equipment from the stores, or for their apparatus to warm up, to sit and think about life. The research man thought to himself, 'I am glad that I am not like some men, or like people of past ages, in bondage to creeds and rules, or even like that student. I have passed my exams. I can beat anyone in an argument and I base my actions on reason alone.'

The other did not trust his thoughts very far. He buried his head in his hands and said, 'God teach me what life is all about. I am ignorant and confused.'

This student learned more than the other, for everyone who is proud of his own intellect will be disillusioned, but the man who is humble enough to seek the truth will find it

*

The framework for this parable is one that was told by Jesus. Like many of his parables it is marked by deliberate caricature and humour. But in the caricature we may see ourselves! The New Testament writer says that Jesus' parable was aimed at those who were sure of their own goodness and looked down on everyone else. Here the principle has been applied to knowledge instead of to righteousness, for there are some who are confident of their own understanding and despise those endowed with lesser brains. If we are to find the truth

. . . to sit and think about life.

about God we must be open to receive his revelation of himself: intellectually humble rather than intellectually proud.

'There's none so blind as they that won't see,' wrote Swift in his *Polite conversation* two and a half centuries ago, giving a phrase that many have quoted (sometimes in a manner rather less than polite!). When knowledge of a truth demands a fundamental change in our attitudes and life-style there is much more controversy about it than about knowledge of things that do not affect us so much. Arguments about the nature of moral responsibility in science provide one example of this: some of those who voice their opinions most strongly are those with most at stake.

When talking with his critics Jesus said that those who were willing to obey the truth would find it. In moral issues, knowledge of the truth makes demands upon us and a willingness to obey the truth when it is found can be a condition for finding it.

There is some hesitation in most of us when it comes to knowing the truth about ourselves, or the truth about God. In part there is a fear that the discovery of God will mean coming under his direction. Such fears are foolish fears, for Christians of all ages bear witness to the love of God and declare that he knows better what is good for us than we could ever know ourselves. They have found that Christian commitment brings a joy and fullness to life. But it is natural to hesitate before trusting our lives to God, even when there is a growing consciousness of the truth about him. How awkward it would be to find God if he wanted us to conform to the 'strait and narrow' path of orthodox behaviour! How embarrassing it might be if we found that he demanded a radical attitude on social questions and the use of our time and money in the service of others!

In the original of the story which we have been considering Jesus spoke about righteousness rather than knowledge. The word righteousness is unfashionable today but fashion can be at fault. Do we really want to know the truth? In order to know the truth we will need to be true in ourselves. We need the righteousness that comes from God's redemption just as much as we need the understanding that comes from God's revelation.

But for those with enquiring minds, who want to obey the truth when they find it, the message of Jesus Christ has its own power to bring conviction. By reading about Jesus, and by talking with those who already believe in him, a man will come to recognize that Jesus Christ is the living Saviour and Lord. Some suggestions for further reading are given at the end of this book.

20 *The last barrier*

In the Bible it is stated that the last enemy to be destroyed is death. In terms of individual human experience that cannot be denied. But it is true, also, that for many the last barrier to faith is the harsh reality of suffering and death and evil in the world. How can we reconcile such an unhappy world as this with such a good God as the God whom Christians claim to know? One way of putting the problem is that if God is good he wouldn't want men to suffer and that if God is also all-powerful he could stop their suffering.

Christian thinking starts with Christ. Christians understand that in some way the suffering and death of Jesus Christ was expected and necessary and that it forms part of God's plan for creation. The whole of Scripture speaks of man's responsibility to God and presupposes that man is free to choose and is responsible for his decisions. Man is not programmed into compulsory obedience to God, because the greatest good is the freedom to love God or to reject him. Only with that freedom can the relationship between man and God be one of reciprocal love and fellowship.

Next comes the heart of the argument: that God 'could not' both give man real freedom and control his response. It sounds like blasphemy yet I think it's true. It is in line with the claim of Scripture that God 'could not' tell a lie. Perhaps you want to object that, earlier in this book, we argued against the view that thought the miraculous to be impossible; yet now we are claiming that something is impossible, even for God! But while it is wrong to suppose things to be impossible because we cannot understand them, it is surely right to think them impossible when we see clear contradictions in meaning. You can conceive of an all-powerful God? Do you think God could create mountains without valleys? Perhaps God could not create good without the possibility of evil. Love and responsibility depend upon freedom and choice. I find this line of argument satisfying but I know that some may not, and I do not want to suggest that Christianity offers a set of easy answers. Nor will I spend time developing this argument further. We cannot reasonably demand that we should understand and approve all God's actions before we will trust him, for that would be presumption indeed.

However much or however little we may understand of the theory, faith in Jesus Christ is trust in one who shared the conflict and suffering of men and women. His enemies laughed with scorn, his friends deserted him, the religious leaders of his own nation plotted to kill him and the local agents of an alien power put him to death. Faith in Christ, we claim, is compatible with our experience of life in this divided world. Jesus suffered very much, and faith in him is compatible with our suffering and the intense suffering we see in others. Jesus was victorious over suffering and death, and faith in him is compatible with our longing for a better world. Knowing Jesus as Lord goes with a world-view in which we are free to choose and responsible for our own decisions. There are false 'Christianities' that stress one facet of Christian truth into an artificial idealism far removed from the realities of life, but the real Christian faith of the New Testament, centred in Christ, is supremely compatible with our experience of life as it is.

Is there something surprising in this compatibility between Christ and the creation? It's not surprising when we recognize him as the unique Son of the Creator, worthy of our trust, our love and our worship.

IV.

Outward

Christian geometry is a little odd. God is our Father in heaven, yet he is not far from any one of us and in him we live and move and have our being. The Bible-writers refer to the Christian believer as being 'in Christ' but also to 'Christ in you, the hope of glory'.

This is parable-language. It may not be easy to draw the diagrams but the meaning is clear. God is different from us but not remote. And this infinite yet personal God offers us a close personal relationship with himself through Christ.

⊒1 *Way out*

'Man is born to trouble', it says in the book of Job, 'as the sparks (or flames) fly upwards.' Job's comforter observed that it is just as natural for men to find unhappiness and disaster as it is for hot air to rise. Can we disagree? The struggling tribes and states of past ages fighting their environment and each other have given place to a global village, but the troubles remain. Jesus warned his followers to expect wars, famines and other disasters and he was right. Even the good things turn sour, like health programmes leading to population explosions, unemployment, hunger and violence. But often the motives are *not* good. There is still exploitation and injustice in the world and the tools of greed have been sharpened by technology.

Individual experience mirrors the complex dis-ease of our race. Sometimes we try to do good and get into a horrible mess for our pains, hurting others when we mean to help them. Sometimes our motives are wrong and on reflection we are ashamed. We have been driven by selfishness or we have lost our tempers or spoken unkindly and untruthfully. To be human is to know remorse! Any attempts to ease our guilt leave us even more confused if they deny us responsibility for our actions. We accuse others of greed and malice and cannot make excuses for ourselves that we do not allow for them. Guilt is not eased by pretending that the offence does not matter, nor by the patronizing assurance that we could not have done better; but by knowing we have been forgiven by those we have wronged.

How can we find relief from our confusion and guilt? Jesus spoke of two ways out of a troubled existence. One, he said, is a broad way on which it is easy to travel but which leads to destruction. All those distractions that enable us to forget life's troubles and to escape from our responsibilities and burdens form a broad way with the appearance of a main road (and I visualize it leading gently downhill) but it's a dead end! There is also a narrow way. Jesus said that few would find it and that the going would be rough, but that it leads to life.

Jesus spoke of himself as the way. After telling his friends that he was going to heaven to prepare a place for them (pretty shattering that; imagine one of your friends whose integrity and sanity you respected saying that to you) he added:

'I am the way, and the truth, and the life; no one comes to the Father, but by me.'

The early Christians were known as followers of 'the Way'. They used the simile of a journey to describe the Christian life, speaking of Jesus Christ in allegorical confusion but with real meaning as their guide, companion, route and destination. In *Pilgrim's progress* John Bunyan later developed an allegory of the way and gave it added popularity. Christ's way is a way out from the maze of confusion that depicts the human situation. He lifts men and women 'up', out of the maze in a dimension of which they were previously unaware, to see this life in the context of an eternal relationship with the Father-God. Every wrong against our fellow men is a sin against God and Jesus Christ offers the assurance of God's forgiveness. Jesus Christ is the way out of our corporate confusion and our individual distress.

ⵝⵝ *The only way?*

Jesus claimed to be the way to God and also to be the *only* way to God, 'no one comes to the Father, but by me'. When Christians claim that God loves the whole world and then limit the possibility of an eternal relationship with him to the minority of the human race that has heard of Jesus Christ, there are many who would object. In discussing science and faith I have found, time and time again, that questions are asked about the 'fate' of those who have not heard of Christ (and that despite the fact that such questions might be thought peripheral to the theme).

In fact most Christians do not believe that acceptance with God is limited to those who actually speak the name of Christ. For a start the heroes of Old Testament times did not know that name. There are hints in Scripture that all those who wholeheartedly fear God and trust him for mercy are accepted by him. It is hardly surprising that God's dealings with those who have not heard of his special agreement with his people are not described in detail in the Bible since, in the nature of things, those who hear the message of the Bible know about God and about his acts of redemption.

But if Jesus Christ said 'no one comes to the Father, but by me', how can the Christian believe that God accepts some who have never heard of Christ? There is not really any contradiction. A sick man can be healed by a surgeon's skill without knowing the name of the surgeon. He need only submit himself to the surgeon's knife. A man's debt can be settled by a friend who keeps his identity secret. He has but to accept the gracious offer. A man can be forgiven because Christ has died even though he has never heard Christ's name. He has to throw himself on God's mercy and accept whatever means God has decreed shall be used to forgive him. The Bible teaches us that God actually worked through the death and resurrection of Jesus Christ to reconcile men to himself. This was not only a demonstration of God's love but an action by which God changed the relationship between men and himself.

This does not mean that God is satisfied by the man who thinks, 'I'll do my best and leave the rest to God.' Far from it! He warned that many would say, 'Lord, Lord,' but be rejected for their insincerity. Those who have a genuine trust in God will seek to know the truth about him and will recognize Jesus as Lord if they do eventually hear of him. The Bible speaks of those from outside God's covenant with Israel who were accepted by him as 'God-fearers' and tells us also that 'the fear of the Lord is the beginning of wisdom'. In Jesus Christ the true light that enlightens everyone came into the world.

I am afraid that one reason why this question, about the 'fate' of those who have not heard of Christ, is so popular is the hope that we too may be all right even if we ignore him. No! We cannot pretend that we trust God for mercy and then disregard the claims of Christ when we have heard of him. Jesus said of the Pharisees, the religious hypocrites of his day, 'If I had not come and spoken to them, they would not be guilty of sin; but now they have no excuse for their sin.' He could say with equal justification to any irreligious hypocrites of this age that if they were really looking for the truth and willing to take the consequences of belief they would recognize him; 'If they had never heard of me, they would not be guilty of ignoring and rejecting me; but now they have no excuse for their ignorance.'

⊒∃ *Countdown*

... Two, One, Zero. Everything is checked during the countdown and at zero the rocket is fired. Then it achieves the purpose for which it was made and rises to launch the satellite into space. Sometimes during the countdown a fault occurs and a button marked 'abort' is pressed.

There is a countdown to belief. 'Two' can represent a second-hand faith. One child is brought up in a Christian home. At home and church, and perhaps at school, he hears about God and Jesus, about creation and the ten commandments, about the parables and miracles. He believes these things because he believes what he is told by his parents, his pastor and his teachers. His belief in God is secondary because it is derived from his trust in the people around him. But it is not only religious faith that can be second-hand. Denial of faith can be second-hand too. Many people today accept the view of their contemporaries that religion can be ignored and that reports of the miraculous have been discredited. To follow the fashion can mean, all too often, an uncritical acceptance of the beliefs of others.

'One.' Many people question the religious

beliefs of their childhood. 'Is life after death possible? Is it true that God commands us to do some things and not to do others?' This can lead them to a denial and rejection of religious belief and practice. They are confident of their own intellectual powers, often supposing that something is possible only if it is within their understanding. On moral issues there may be a similar rejection of outside authority, an assertion that we are free to do as we please, or at least that we are as good as we need to be. In this way a man has faith in himself, faith in 'number one'.

'Zero.' To many men there comes a time of crisis: to some it is an awareness of our appalling ignorance; to some a sense of moral failure, corruption and guilt; to some it is an experience of alienation, that feeling of being in the wrong place at the wrong time and at odds with everybody and everything. One man may be frustrated when confronted with human need; another may feel angry without knowing the cause for his anger. There may be disillusion from the discovery that those whose views we trusted were themselves ignorant and lost. 'What am I made for? What should I do? How can I know? Where is God?' When men ask such questions in real concern and anguish, and not just out of curiosity, then they have come to an end of themselves, to zero, and they are ready to find God.

'FIRE!' Men start the Christian life in different ways (and often without the noise and

excitement that the comparison with a rocket launching suggests) but it involves in some measure the 'no' of repentance, or turning from themselves, and the 'yes' of trust and commitment. A force of gravity has held them down, so that their thoughts were earthbound and their best endeavours failed. Now they have a new confidence in God and a certitude about the supremacy of Jesus Christ, who frees men for the purpose for which they were made, bringing a new way of thinking and a new style of living. It's a journey to heaven that is more 'above' than above: life in a new dimension.

Two, one, zero. Where are you on the countdown?

ᒧᒡ The travellers

Parables are not analogies. We may compare the
Christian life with a way out from a maze or a journey
into space, but it does not follow that the Christian
leaves this world and its troubles behind. Not yet!
Christians should not be way out from the world by
their distance from it but by the differences they display;
not separated into religious ghettos but distinguished by
Christ-centred thinking and Christ-like behaviour. The
Christian understands that he belongs to God, and that
God's heaven is his eternal home, but he knows also
that God came into this world in Jesus Christ and that it
is in this world, now, that God is to be found and
obeyed. The man who knows he is safe should be ready
to take risks.

Paul the apostle told the early Christians that they
should walk by God's Spirit and, mixing his metaphors,
that the fruit of God's Spirit in a human life includes
love, joy, peace, kindness and self-control. Love? It is
love for God, shown in prayer and worship and
obedience. It is also love for others, not self-centred
possessive lust but a self-giving, in tune with the love
that gave Jesus Christ to the world. This love, God's
love in us creating a love for others, can transform
human relationships, bringing joy and peace into our
homes and into the places where we work. When those
who share the conscious experience of God's love get
together they enjoy the fellowship that characterizes any

truly Christian church or community. The man who knows God's love can afford to love his fellows.

Christians have a responsibility to the world, for it is God's world, but Christian thinking about society and its needs is fundamentally different from the attitudes of those who do not take God into their reckoning. The Christian asks about God's purposes and has a special insight into the nature of man. Man has dignity as God's creature, made in God's likeness: and the Christian opposes those who exploit their fellows, or subject them to dehumanizing conditions of work in the interests of 'economies of scale', or feed them with false information. But man is fallen, diseased with sin and a source of contamination to others: and the Christian takes issue with those who exalt man and teach that he should be allowed to be his unbridled self, or that the *only* change needed is a change in social structure. That is a recipe for disaster, for men need to be protected from themselves and from each other, not by despotic power but by an ordering of society that is itself restrained.

The Christian is often in conflict with contemporary ideas, but he knows that history is littered with accounts of ideas and policies that seemed compelling in their time and met their doom because they did not take proper account of human nature and the workings of the world. Scientific thinking is self-correcting and it must accord with the facts if it is to stand the test of time. Because of this the Christian will not *necessarily* reach different conclusions from those of his non-Christian colleagues. Although the Christian has a different basis for his thinking it does not follow that there need be a 'Christian' ecology or a 'Christian' sociology or a 'Christian' political party. It is possible for people to reach the same conclusions on questions of policy even though they hold views on fundamental issues that are irreconcilable, just as special relativity and Newtonian mechanics give identical predictions in many cases despite a fundamental difference between them. Human ideas are constrained by the facts of life. The demand that they be compatible with the world as it is ensures a measure of consensus. A *right* understanding of some part of the creation will not conflict with a *right* understanding of the Creator.

Two warnings are needed. Different Christians are called to serve God in different ways and we should not be too hasty in our judgement on those whose priorities are different from ours. The need for the second warning is obvious from history. It is that sincere and devout Christians can be silly and prejudiced in their thinking. That's not the way Christ means them to be, but he doesn't force his will on any of us. In one way or another we all abuse the freedom of thought and action that God has given.

For God has set us in a dangerous place. He wills it so, for the goal makes the risk worth while. He offers us the Spirit, the reality, of Jesus Christ as a promise that we shall reach the goal and have strength and wisdom on the way. Jesus knows the dangers. And the glory.

25 *Guidelines*

It has been my aim in this short book to show that there is a way out from the closed thinking of our age and that the way out is Jesus Christ. Five short sentences could sum it up.

There is more to life than science or technology might suggest.

The unusual and the unexpected are not necessarily impossible.

New ideas may be tested by asking if they are compatible with what we know already.

God is speaking: we shall 'hear' him when we are ready to obey him.

Jesus Christ offers us a way out to a new and eternal life.

Parables and analogies with what we know already are necessary to introduce us to such new ideas and new life. A short introduction has served its purpose if it whets the reader's appetite for more. What will you read next? The bookfinder chart gives some suggestions, listed below, but it may be necessary to go to a library for books that are currently out of print.

Book list

1. Edwin A. Abbott, *Flatland, a romance of many dimensions*, second edition 1884, Blackwell (also Dover paperback in USA); also Barnes and Noble, New York, 5th revised edition, 1969.

2. Sir Norman Anderson, *Christianity and comparative religion*, IVP, 1970.

3. Ian G. Barbour, *Issues in science and religion*, SCM Press, 1966; also Harper and Row, 1971. This is an excellent historical survey of some 470 pages, almost a standard text. Near the end of the book, Barbour suggests a model for the relationship between God and the world based on 'process theology' and many may think this does not allow sufficient recognition of the power and supremacy of God. But Barbour's analysis of different viewpoints is concise and fair, his chapter summaries excellent and his book a scholarly work in readable style. There are numerous references and an index. This book is currently out of print in the UK.

4. Oliver R. Barclay, *Reasons for faith*, IVP, 1974.

5. R. T. France, *The man they crucified*, IVP, 1975.

6. Os Guinness, *The dust of death*, IVP, 1973.

7. M. A. Jeeves, *Psychology and Christianity: the view both ways*, IVP, 1976.

8. C. S. Lewis, *Till we have faces*, Geoffrey Bles, 1956, but out of print, is an allegory. *Out of the silent planet*, *Voyage to Venus* (originally published as *Perelandra*) and *That hideous strength*, all in Pan paperback, are science fiction.

9. C. S. Lewis, *Mere Christianity*, Fontana paperback, 1970, an easily read and persuasive presentation of Christian belief.

10. C. S. Lewis, *The problem of pain*, Fontana paperback, 1957, a general book on the subject, and *A grief observed*, Faber, 1966, a personal account written after the death of his wife.

11. D. Lyon, *Christians and sociology*, IVP, 1975.

12. D. M. MacKay, *The clockwork image*, IVP, 1974.

MacKay has pioneered the use of the complementary concept in expressing the relationship between faith and science. Chapters eight and nine of *The clockwork image* are concerned with determinism and freedom. I do not find them wholly convincing, perhaps I do not fully understand them, but MacKay's main conclusions do not seem, to me, to depend on the arguments in these two chapters.

13. D. S. Spanner, *Creation and evolution*, Falcon Press, 1965.
14. J. R. W. Stott, *Basic Christianity*, IVP second edition, 1971. A thorough introduction to the Christian faith.
15. J. R. W. Stott, *Understanding the Bible*, Scripture Union, 1972.
16. John Wenham, *The goodness of God*, IVP, 1974.

*

But the source-book is the Bible. I am not sure that my Christian friends (who ought to read it often) realize what a strange book it seems to those reading it for the first time or who have not read it since they were children. It's worth using a modern version, for the 'thee's' and 'thou's' of sixteenth-century English have nothing to do with the intentions of the original writers. But the Bible is anchored in history. When Jesus says he is the good shepherd we shall understand him better if we learn about the customs of shepherds in Palestine at that time. The study of the Bible requires some study of its background.

Unfortunately there are many books about the Bible that will *not* help us to understand it. A number of contemporary theologians accept unquestioningly a nineteenth-century view of science. They imagine that miracles and prophecies about future events are impossible.

They edit the Bible accordingly, rejecting as invention rather than true report those parts describing the miraculous. Their understanding of the Bible's message is distorted by their misunderstanding of science and their conclusions throw more light on their own thinking than on the object of their study. Such criticism is not a condemnation of all scholarly study of Christian scripture, only a warning that the conclusions reached will depend on the presuppositions that are made.

The Bible does not give a systematic analysis of the human condition or a systematic theology requiring only an intellectual study: it tells of a personal God acting in the lives of particular people and thus enables us to find and know this God for ourselves. God is described as holy and righteous, setting standards for our lives and giving directions of which we have been ignorant or which, to our shame, we have known but ignored. The Bible tells of God's love, that makes God *ask* for our obedience but not compel it, and of his answer to human disobedience when the demands of holiness and love are reconciled by God's own act in the death and resurrection of Jesus Christ.

Who, really, is this Jesus? If we are to know the answer to that question for ourselves we must 'meet' him and recognize him. Faith in Jesus Christ is not a funny feeling but a recognition that brings with it acceptance of his friendship, his forgiveness and his supremacy. We shall never see the significance of a pattern if we do not give it our attention; we shall never get to know Jesus Christ unless we give ourselves (and him!) a chance. One of the best ways of doing this is to read, or to read over again, one of the Gospel accounts that describe the significance of his life and message.

There follows a list of Bible references that are quoted

in different sections of this book or are relevant to them as background reading. This could serve as an introduction to the Bible.

Chapter	Theme	References
2	Some parables of Jesus	Matthew 13; Luke 15.
7	Idols	Isaiah 44 (especially verses 9–17).
Section II	Impossible?	Luke 18:27
8	Through closed doors	John 20:19–23.
11	Eternal life	John 17:3; Luke 20:27–38; 1 Corinthians 15.
12	God upholds	Hebrews 1:1–4; Psalm 19.
13	God is 'no where'	Job 23.
	Paul preaching in Athens	Acts 17:16–34.
15	Knowing God	Matthew 11:25–30; Romans 10:17; 1 Corinthians 2.
17, 18	Seeing Jesus as Lord	Mark 8:11–38; Luke 24:13–35; John 20:11–31. (Remember Matthew 13:14–17).
19	Two attitudes	Luke 18:9–14.
20	Christ's death	Hebrews 9:27, 28; 1 Peter 1:18–21; Luke 22:31–23:49; Matthew 28.
	God cannot lie	Titus 1:1–4; Hebrews 6:17, 18; 1 Samuel 15:29.
Section IV	'In Christ in you'	Colossians 1:27, 28.
21	Trouble	Job 5:6, 7; Matthew 24:3–8.
	The Way	Matthew 7:13, 14; John 14:1–6; Acts 9:1–6.
22	God's mercy	Luke 1:50; Acts 10:34, 35.
	Christ's work	2 Corinthians 5:17–21.
	No excuses	Matthew 7:21 27; Proverbs 1:7; John 1:9; John 15:22.
23	Yes and no	Mark 1:14, 15; See also 1 John 1:9.
24	In the world, not of it	John 17:14–18; Philippians 3:20; John 3:16.
	Paul's metaphors	Galatians 5:16, 22, 25.
	Power to love	Romans 5:5; 1 John 4:19–21.
	Man's dignity	Genesis 1:27; Psalm 8; Ephesians 4:13.
	Man's fall	Genesis 6:5, 6; Romans 3:23.
	Exploitation	James 4:13–5:6.
	Rulers	Romans 13:1–7; Acts 5:29.
	Different callings	1 Corinthians 12:4–14:1.
	The Spirit of Christ	Ephesians 1:13, 14; Romans 8.

Bookfinder

A. Faith and science

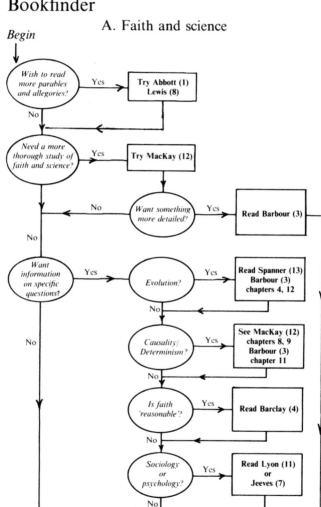

Begin

Wish to read more parables and allegories? — **Yes** → **Try Abbott (1) Lewis (8)**

No

Need a more thorough study of faith and science? — **Yes** → **Try MacKay (12)**

Want something more detailed? — **Yes** → **Read Barbour (3)**

No

No

Want information on specific questions? — **Yes** →

Evolution? — **Yes** → **Read Spanner (13) Barbour (3) chapters 4, 12**

No

Causality/ Determinism? — **Yes** → **See MacKay (12) chapters 8, 9 Barbour (3) chapter 11**

No

Is faith 'reasonable'? — **Yes** → **Read Barclay (4)**

No

Sociology or psychology? — **Yes** → **Read Lyon (11) or Jeeves (7)**

No

No

B. Christian belief

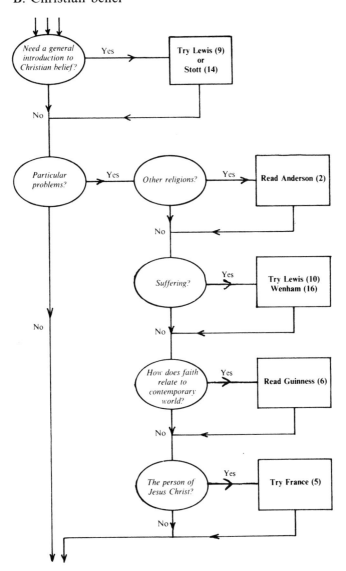

C. The Bible

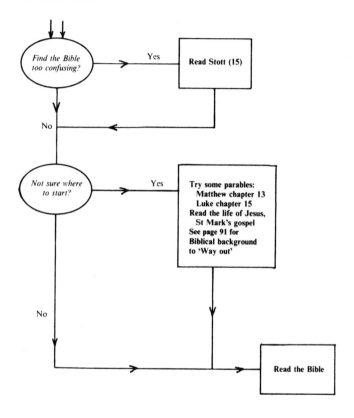

'If you continue in my word, you are truly my disciples, and you will know the truth, and the truth will make you free.'

Jesus Christ (John 8:32)

Postscript

I should like to record my thanks to all those who have stimulated my thinking about the relationship between faith and science. I owe a special debt to the many students in Africa and elsewhere with whom I have discussed the subject and whose questions and arguments have helped to shape what I have written.

Denis Osborne

London 1977